FOREST FIGHTER

THE STORY OF CHICO MENDES

Anita Ganeri   Margaux Carpentier

Crocodile   Books, USA

An imprint of Interlink Publishing Group, Inc.

www.interlinkbooks.com

First published in 2022 by
Crocodile Books
An imprint of Interlink Publishing Group, Inc.
46 Crosby Street, Northampton, MA 01060
www.interlinkbooks.com

Published simultaneously in the UK by Wayland, an imprint of Hachette Children's Group

Managing editor: Victoria Brooker
Design: Anthony Hannant, Little Red Ant

Library of Congress Cataloging-in-Publication data:
Names: Ganeri, Anita, 1961- author. | Carpentier, Margaux, illustrator.
Title: Forest fighter : the story of Chico Mendes / Anita Ganeri, Margaux Carpentier.
Description: Northampton: Crocodile Books, an Imprint of Interlink Publishing Group, Inc., 2022. | Audience: Ages 7 to 12 | Identifiers: LCCN 2021062638 |
ISBN 9781623718565 (hardback); 9781623718183 (paperback)
Subjects: LCSH: Mendes, Chico, -1988—Juvenile literature. | Conservationists—Brazil—Biography—Juvenile literature. | Rubber tappers—Brazil—Biography—Juvenile literature. | Rain forest conservation—Amazon River Region—Juvenile literature. | Deforestation—Amazon River Region—Juvenile literature. | BISAC: JUVENILE NONFICTION / Biography & Autobiography / Social Activists | JUVENILE NONFICTION / People & Places / United States / Hispanic & Latino
Classification: LCC SD411.52.M46 G36 2022 | DDC 333.72092 [B]—dc2320220104
LC record available at https://lccn.loc.gov/2021062638.

Printed and bound in China
10 9 8 7 6 5 4 3 2

Contents

Fighters for the forest

The birds had stopped singing. Instead, the whine of chainsaws filled the air. In a clearing in the Amazon rainforest, a large group of men, women, and children watched in horror, as tree after tree crashed to the ground. Wealthy cattle ranchers wanted this land for pasture and would stop at nothing to get it. The group was led by a man called Chico Mendes, a poor rubber tapper like the rest. For years, he had led the struggle for fairer treatment of the tappers, and to protect the forest they relied on for their living.

Sensing trouble, the ranchers had already called the police, who now raised their guns. Immediately, the women and children moved to the front of the group. The police could not now open fire. Then, an amazing thing happened—first the women and children, then the whole group, started to sing the national anthem of Brazil. Out of respect, the police were forced to lower their weapons, stand to attention, and salute. When the singing ended, Chico stepped forward. Softly-spoken and calm, he asked for the cutting to be halted for the day. Caught by surprise, the police agreed.

It was a small victory in a very long battle to save the rainforest—a battle that, one day, would cost Chico his life.

Born in the forest

Francisco Alves Mendes Filho, known as Chico (*Shee-koh*), was born on December 15, 1944. His parents, Francisco and Irace, lived deep in the Amazon rainforest, not far from the small town of Xapuri (*Shah-poo-ree*) in the state of Acre, in western Brazil.

Francisco and Irace came from families who arrived in Acre from the northeast, some years before. Their own parents had made the long journey by steamboat, in the hope of starting a new and better life as tappers on a rubber estate—a large area of rainforest where rubber trees grew wild.

The Mendes family was one of many families who moved into the forest at that time. The estate owners gave each a patch of rubber trees, and the tools needed for tapping. The Mendes family's patch was called Bom Futuro ("Good Future" in Portuguese). They hoped that it would live up to its name.

Starting work

When Chico was around eight years old, he began to go to work with his father, and to learn how to tap. Early in the morning, they set off into the forest. At each rubber tree, Francisco showed Chico how to cut a slant in the bark with a hooked knife. Then he fixed a tin cup, or a Brazil nut pod, under the cut to collect the latex (white liquid) that oozed out.

Rubber tappers like Francisco knew how to collect latex without doing the trees any long-term harm. Trees were tapped, then left alone for several years to rest and heal. This way, the tappers could make their living while keeping the forest healthy.

Afterward, Chico and his father went hunting for animals, such as tapirs, armadillos, and monkeys, for the cooking pot. Chico loved hunting and quickly learned where to find animals from their feeding habits and hiding places.

Busy afternoons

After a quick lunch of rice and beans, Chico and Francisco retraced their steps to collect the latex from the trees they'd tapped. Back home, they cured the latex by heating it over a smoky fire so that it turned into a hard, rubber ball, ready for sale. It was a horrible job. The smoke made their eyes sting and also made them cough.

Chico and his father went out tapping three to four times a week. They walked many miles each time. When the rainy season made tapping difficult, they harvested Brazil nuts to sell instead. The nuts grew inside hard, baseball-sized pods on towering Brazil nut trees, some of the tallest trees in the rainforest. They could only be collected when the pods fell to the ground. The tappers could then hack off the tops with machetes.

Deep in debt

By the time he turned 11, Chico was rubber-tapping full time. His family moved to a different rubber estate. Each estate was owned by a wealthy businessman. At the end of each season, the tappers sold their rubber to the estate owner. He weighed it, and paid them for it, but only after he'd taken payment for the tools he'd given them, and rent for the trees. By the time he'd finished, there was very little money left for the tappers.

While the estate owners grew richer and richer, the rubber tappers stayed poor and deeply in debt. In fact, they were being cheated out of a fair reward for their hard work. The owners did not want tappers exchanging stories about how unfair this was. They made sure that families were scattered about the forest, several hours' walk apart. They also offered rewards for tappers to spy on each other so that they didn't know who to trust.

Forest school

Chico loved the rainforest. He said it felt like part of him and was where he was happiest. Chico got to know the rainforest like the back of his hand. He learned the names of the trees, and how to tell them apart by sniffing their bark. He learned which plants were useful for food and medicines, and which were poisonous. He learned to recognize many birds and animals by their calls alone.

Chico did not go to school. Schools were not allowed on the rubber estates. The owners didn't want tappers to be able to read, write, and do math in case they worked out how the owners were cheating them. No school also meant that children were free to work, meaning bigger profits for the owners. Unusually for a tapper, Francisco could read a bit. Most evenings, he and Chico sat on the veranda. By the light of a smoky oil lamp, Francisco taught his son what he knew.

A stranger arrives

One evening, a stranger turned up at Chico's house. His name was Euclides Fernandes Tavora. He had a newspaper stuffed into his pocket. Chico had never seen a newspaper before and was curious. Noticing his interest, Tavora said he would be happy to teach Chico to read and write. Francisco agreed that Chico could take time off work on the weekends. So, every Saturday afternoon for several months, Chico walked for three hours through the forest to Tavora's hut for lessons. He spent the weekend there, then headed home on Monday to work.

With no textbooks, Tavora used newspapers to teach Chico. Often these papers were months out of date, but that didn't matter. It wasn't very long before Chico could read and write fluently.

Teaching and politics

Chico's lessons with Tavora changed his life. Now that he could read and write, Tavora urged him to use his skills in the struggle for the rubber tappers' rights. From his own experience, Chico knew how unfairly the tappers were treated. However hard he and his own family worked, they were still miserably poor.

Tavora also talked to Chico about politics, at home and around the world. At that time, a very strict military government ruled Brazil. Anyone who criticized the government could be arrested, and many people suffered. While a few Brazilians grew richer and more powerful, many more were plunged deeper into poverty.

Chico got a job at the Brazilian Literacy Movement, teaching adults how to read and write. Most of his students were rubber tappers. From them, Chico learned even more about the problems that they faced.

Opening the Amazon

The Amazon is the biggest rainforest on Earth, roughly the size of Australia. More than half of the forest grows in Brazil and it is home to an incredible variety of wildlife. Scientists estimate that around one in ten of all known species of animals and plants lives there. For many people in Brazil, though, the rainforest was a wild, faraway place. They didn't think about it, or know very much about it.

In the 1970s, all of this began to change. The government urgently needed money and turned its attention to the Amazon. They wanted cattle ranchers to come to the region. The plan was for the ranchers to clear large areas of forest and turn it into pasture for cattle. Beef from the cattle could be sold abroad, bringing much-needed funds into the country. By now, sales of rubber had slumped. Many rubber estate owners were only too happy to sell their land to the ranchers, for a big profit.

Roads to ruin

The government also started building new roads through the Amazon. Huge areas of precious forest were cut down and burned on either side. The roads brought thousands of new settlers into the forest. Many were workers from cities in the south. The government promised them plots of land for farming, houses, schools, and medical care. But the settlers' dreams didn't last long.

Without tree roots to bind it together, the rainforest soil is poor. Once the land was cleared, ready for planting crops, the soil quickly dried up and nothing could grow. Some settlements became overcrowded, and deadly diseases, such as malaria and yellow fever, took hold. With no other way of earning a living, the settlers were worse off than before. Many were forced to move out of the forest and into a miserable life in the city slums.

Forest people

Many rubber estates had now been sold to ranchers. They wanted the land cleared, quickly, and that meant the rubber tappers had to go. If the tappers refused to leave, the ranchers threatened them and burned down their huts. The tappers faced losing both their homes and their living. Collecting rubber and Brazil nuts was all they knew. But they were poor people and the ranchers were rich and powerful. What could the tappers do?

Around them, they watched the rainforest burn. In just five years, approximately 180,000 rubber trees and 80,000 Brazil nut trees were destroyed close to where Chico lived. At first, ash from the burned trees made the soil rich for growing grass. But this only lasted for two to three years. Then the ranchers had to move on. To grow enough pasture, more and more forest had to be cleared. Chico knew that if the destruction carried on at this rate, there would soon be no rainforest left.

Taking up the fight

Chico decided that the time had come to speak out on behalf of the rubber tappers and the rainforest they lived in and relied on. But the tappers were scattered widely about the forest, often many miles apart. A Rural Workers' Union (a trade union) was set up and Chico was elected secretary, or spokesperson. It took a lot of courage to stand up to the government. Chico was often in trouble for speaking out against the ranchers and challenging the government's plans for the Amazon. But he was determined to keep up the fight.

A few years later, Chico left the council to become president of the Xapuri union. He spent many days hiking through the rainforest, visiting tappers and their families. He wanted them to join the union, but first he needed to win their trust. So he spent time just sitting and chatting to them, and playing with their children. The tappers liked Chico. He was softly spoken, a good listener, and they knew he was on their side.

Forest protest

The rubber tappers found a new way of protesting. When a rancher began clearing the forest, the tappers called for their neighbors. Then, the tappers and their families lined up in front of the workers and pleaded with them to stop. Very often, the workers listened and put down their chainsaws. This type of protest was called an *empate*, which means "obstacle" in Portuguese. Hundreds were held all over the Amazon, to the ranchers' fury. As tension grew between the two sides, the ranchers turned violent.

On June 21, 1980, a gunman, hired by ranchers, killed Wilson Pinheiro, president of the Rural Workers' Union. Wilson and Chico were close friends and Chico knew he could be the next target.

Spreading the word

Early in 1985, elections were held in Brazil. The military rulers were defeated and a new government voted in. It drew up plans for the Amazon, but ignored the rubber tappers. Disappointed, Chico organized the first-ever meeting of tappers from all over the Amazon. It was held in Brasília, the capital of Brazil, in October. Around 130 tappers traveled for days, by boat, canoe, bus, and on foot to attend. For many, it was their first trip away from home.

At the meeting, Chico also asked for some areas of rainforest to be set aside as "extractive reserves." These reserves would still be owned by the government, but tappers and other forest people would have the right to live and work there, in return for looking after the land. The idea was to show that it was possible to use the rainforest and its valuable resources without destroying it.

Waking up the world

Chico's fame was spreading. In 1987, he was invited to the USA to meet officials from a leading bank. The bank had promised the Brazilian government a loan to build a new road in Acre. Chico wanted guarantees that the road-building would not cause too much damage to the rainforest. The bank put the loan on hold until plans to protect the rainforest were agreed upon.

Later that year, Chico went to England to collect a Global 500 prize. This was awarded by the United Nations Environment Program for Chico's work in protecting the rainforest. A few months later, he was back in the USA to receive a Better World Society award. He dedicated both prizes to the rubber tappers.

Going green

Chico loved the rainforest. He said that the forest felt like part of him, and was where he was happiest. He did not set out to bring the destruction of the rainforest to the world's attention, but his work on behalf of the tappers did just that, and highlighted the danger it was in.

By now, scientists were realizing that destroying the rainforests has effects on the whole planet, not just on local people's lives. Burning rainforest trees releases huge amounts of carbon dioxide into the atmosphere. Trees also soak up carbon dioxide when they photosynthesize. Fewer trees means that this storage system is lost.

Larger amounts of carbon dioxide and other greenhouse gases in the atmosphere are causing the world to become warmer, with dramatic changes to the climate. In addition, the loss of forest is driving countless extraordinary species of animals and plants toward extinction.

Threats of violence

Back in Brazil, politicians were angry. They accused Chico of trying to ruin the country's progress for his own gain. Chico stayed calm. If the politicians were so worried, he said, the rubber tappers must be winning their battle.

Meanwhile, the ranchers began holding cattle auctions, to raise funds for buying guns. They killed several tappers and made threats against Chico's life. Early in 1988, a man called Darli Alves da Silva bought up part of the Cachoeira rubber estate, where Chico had grown up. He began forcing the tappers off the land. For weeks, the tappers staged *empate* after *empate*. They refused to back down, even after Darli sent in gunmen to shoot at them. Under pressure, the government took back the Cachoeira estate and handed it over to the tappers. It became the first extractive reserve in the Amazon.

But Darli hadn't finished with Chico yet.

Fateful day

Chico's friends begged him to leave Xapuri and go into hiding to save his life. He refused, saying that he wasn't afraid and had no plans to run away. On December 15, his wife, Ilza, threw a 44th birthday party for Chico. He and his guests sang, danced, and laughed until late into the night. A friend gave him a blue towel as a present, decorated with musical notes.

Chico was happy to be home for Christmas with his family. On December 22, he took his children for a ride around town in the union's new truck. Later, he sat at his kitchen table, playing dominoes with his two new bodyguards. Ilza was busy cooking fish for dinner and the children were watching TV.

The evening was hot and sticky. Chico decided to head out for a shower and grabbed his new towel. As he opened the back door, two gunmen came out of the bushes and shot him in the chest. Chico stumbled back into the house, but a few minutes later, he died.

Chico's legacy

News of Chico's death spread quickly. On Christmas Day, more than a thousand people crowded into the church in Xapuri for his funeral. Among them were hundreds of rubber tappers who had walked a long way to say goodbye. They were joined by union leaders, politicians, journalists, and environmentalists from all over Brazil. A banner at the funeral read, "Chico Mendes—they have killed our leader, but not our struggle."

In death, Chico became even more famous than he had been when he was alive. Under his quiet but determined leadership, the plight of the Amazon rainforest had become, and remains, an international cause.

CHICO VIVE

A year later, the president of Brazil signed a decree for more of the extractive reserves that Chico had worked so hard for. One such reserve stretched for around 2.5 million acres across Xapuri, Brasiléia, and Rio Branco. It was named after Chico.

Forest future

Today, some 10,000 people live in the Chico Mendes Extractive Reserve. They tap rubber and harvest Brazil nuts. They are also allowed to cut down a set number of trees for timber and clear certain areas for pasture. Despite problems with illegal logging and burning, there is also good news. In 2017, conservationists from the World Wild Fund for Nature (WWF) filmed a family of very rare rodents, called pacaranas, for the first time. The sighting proved that, if the forest is well managed, its precious wildlife will also survive.

Sadly, despite Chico's pioneering work, and pressure from governments and conservationists around the world, the Amazon rainforest has continued to burn. In 2019, there was the greatest loss of forest for ten years, with the equivalent of two soccer fields being cleared every minute. Chico would have been horrified. But he would also have been proud to see that his children are working tirelessly to carry on his struggle and work. Elenira was just four years old when she saw her father murdered. Twenty years later, she continues the work to protect the rainforest and the communities that live there.

CASA DE CHICO MENDES

"At first I thought I was fighting to save rubber trees, then I thought I was fighting to save the Amazon rainforest. Now I realize I am fighting for humanity." Chico Mendes

Amazon rainforest facts

The Amazon is the biggest tropical rainforest in the world. It covers more than 2.1 million sq mi—making it almost twice the size of India.

The Amazon lies mostly in Brazil, South America, but also stretches into Bolivia, Ecuador, Colombia, Peru, Guyana, Suriname, and French Guiana.

The Amazon rainforest is the richest habitat anywhere on Earth. It contains a tenth of all known species of plants and animals found in the world.

The gigantic Amazon river runs through the northern part of the rainforest. The second longest river on Earth (after the Nile), it stretches for 4,250 miles.

In the past twenty years, more than 2,000 new species of plants and animals have been discovered. They include a monkey that purrs like a cat.

The Amazon rainforest is being destroyed at an alarming rate. In the last 40 years alone, around a fifth has been destroyed.

The rainforest is also home to around 350 tribes of indigenous people. Some have never had any contact with the outside world. Others, like the Yanomami, are well known.

A quarter of all the plants we use to make medicines comes from rainforests. Many of them come from the Amazon.

Climate change is having a major effect on the rainforest, including terrible droughts. These can cause crops and fish to die and devastating forest fires to break out.

Around 120 billion tonnes of carbon are stored in Amazon rainforest trees. This helps to stabilize the climate, both locally and around the world.

Glossary

atmosphere mixtures of gases surrounding the Earth

auction sale of goods where people make higher and higher offers of money

carbon dioxide gas formed when carbon is burned, or when people or animals breathe out

chainsaw large saw with a motor, and "teeth" fitted onto a chain

clearing area in a forest where trees and bushes have been cut down

climate weather in a place over a long period of time

conservationist someone who works to protect the environment

cured when latex is heated to turn it into rubber

debt money that is owed to someone else

decree official decision or order

election when people vote to choose a new government

empate form of protest; means "obstacle" in the Portuguese language

environment places where people, animals, and plants live

environmentalist someone who studies the natural environment and tries to protect it

extinction when a plant or animal no longer exists

extractive involved in taking metals, oil, and other resources from the environment

fluently able to speak and read a language quickly and easily

greenhouse gases gases, such as carbon dioxide, in the atmosphere that are causing the Earth's climate to change

guarantee a written promise that something will be done

humanity people in general

illegal against the law

journalist someone who writes or talks about things happening in the news

latex white liquid produced by rubber trees

literacy being able to read and write

loan money that is borrowed

machete large knife with a wide, curved blade

military to do with the armed forces (army, navy, air force)

national anthem official song of a country

pasture grassy land suitable for cattle and sheep

photosynthesize when a plant uses carbon dioxide from the air, water from the ground, and energy from sunlight to make food

pioneering being the first to do something or try something out

politician member of a government or law-making organization

politics actions taken by governments or organizations to change laws

profit money earned from buying and selling things

rent amount of money charged for using something

reserve protected area of land, such as a rainforest

resource a useful or valuable thing

rights being treated in a fair and equal way

rubber tapper someone who collects latex from rubber trees

rubber tapping collecting latex from rubber trees

secretary someone who helps to manage an organization

slums very poor, overcrowded parts of a city

trade union an organization that stands up for workers' rights

Index